The Classical Piano
Sheet Music Series

INTERMEDIATE
J.S. BACH
FAVORITES

ISBN 978-1-70515-239-3

HAL•LEONARD®

Visit Hal Leonard Online at
www.halleonard.com

Contact us:
Hal Leonard
7777 West Bluemound Road
Milwaukee, WI 53213
Email: info@halleonard.com

In Europe, contact:
Hal Leonard Europe Limited
1 Red Place
London, W1K 6PL
Email: info@halleonardeurope.com

In Australia, contact:
Hal Leonard Australia Pty. Ltd.
4 Lentara Court
Cheltenham, Victoria, 3192 Australia
Email: info@halleonard.com.au

Contents

SELECTED PRELUDES

Invention No. 1 in C Major
BWV 772

Johann Sebastian Bach
(1685–1750)

Invention No. 2 in C minor
BWV 773

Johann Sebastian Bach
(1685–1750)

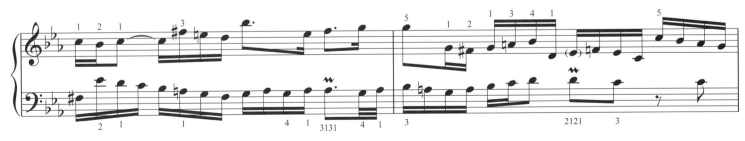

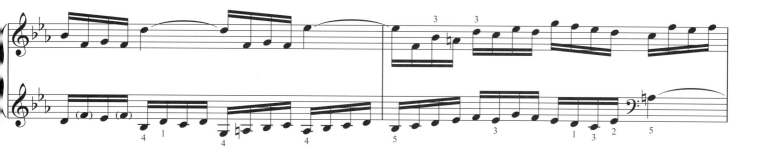

Invention No. 3 in D Major
BWV 774

Johann Sebastian Bach
(1685–1750)

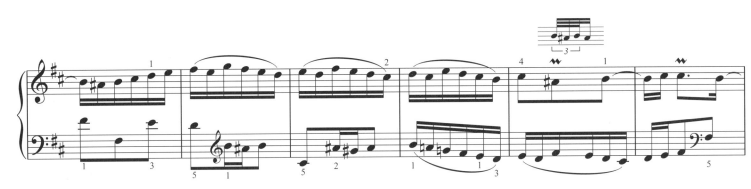

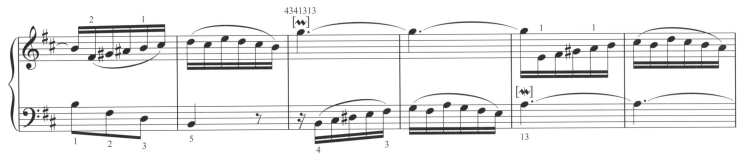

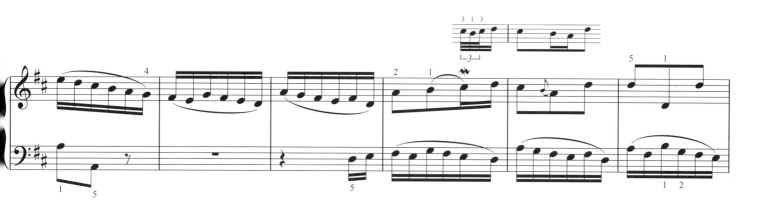

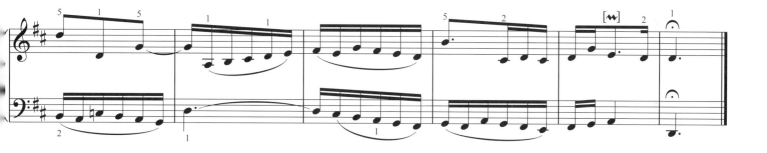

Invention No. 4 in D minor
BWV 775

Johann Sebastian Bach
(1685–1750)

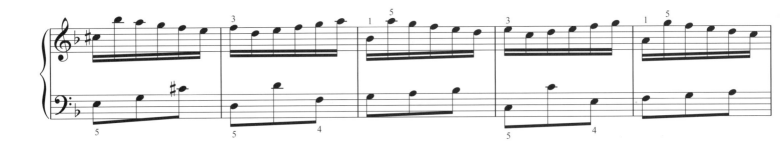

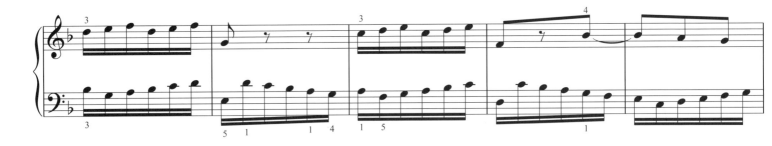

Invention No. 5 in E-flat Major
BWV 776

Johann Sebastian Bach
(1685–1750)

Invention No. 6 in E Major
BWV 777

Johann Sebastian Bach
(1685–1750)

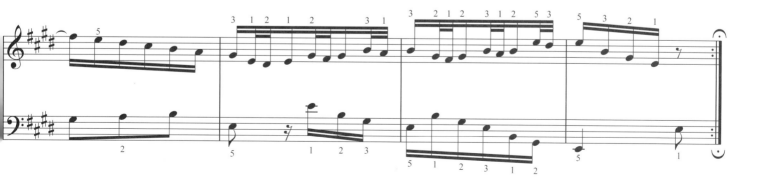

Invention No. 7 in E minor
BWV 778

Johann Sebastian Bach
(1685–1750)

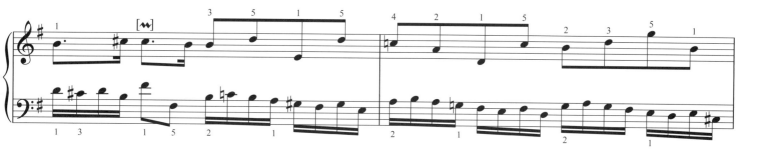

Invention No. 8 in F Major
BWV 779

Johann Sebastian Bach
(1685–1750)

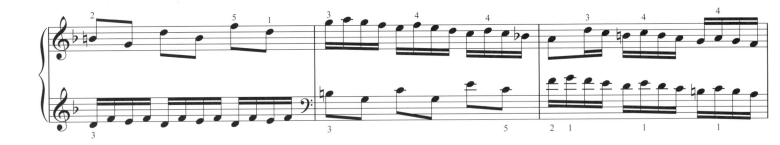

Invention No. 9 in F minor
BWV 780

Johann Sebastian Bach
(1685–1750)

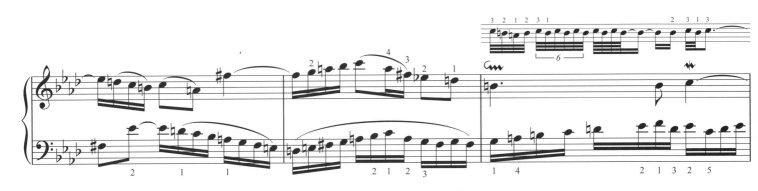

Invention No. 10 in G Major
BWV 781

Johann Sebastian Bach
(1685–1750)

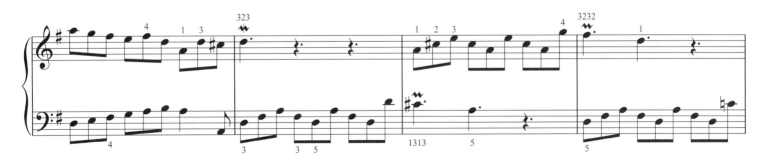

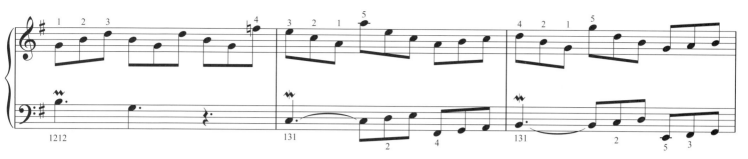

Invention No. 11 in G minor
BWV 782

Johann Sebastian Bach
(1685–1750)

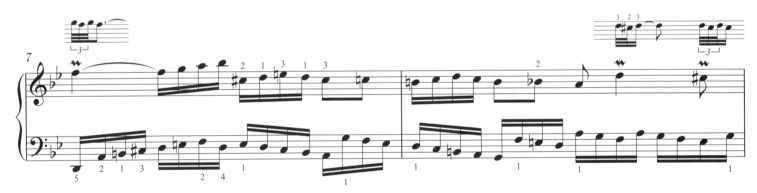

Invention No. 12 in A Major
BWV 783

Johann Sebastian Bach
(1685–1750)

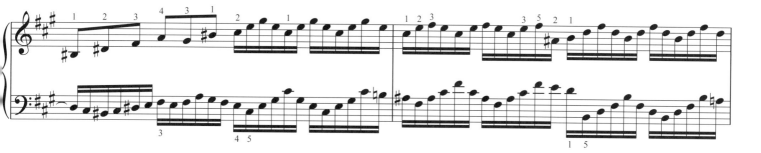

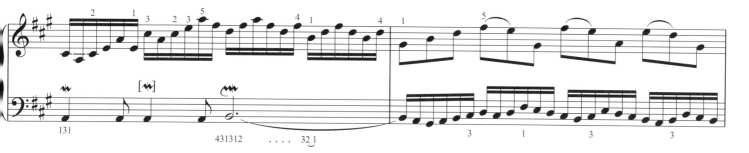

Invention No. 13 in A minor
BWV 784

Johann Sebastian Bach
(1685–1750)

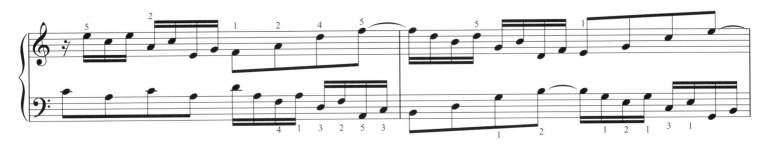

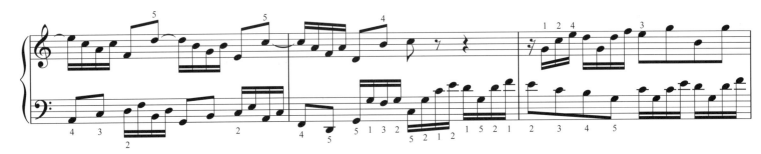

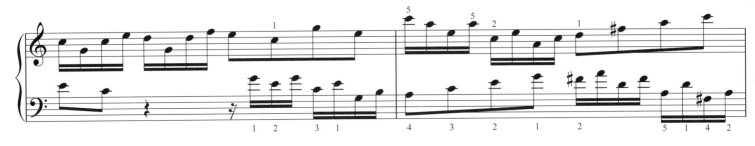

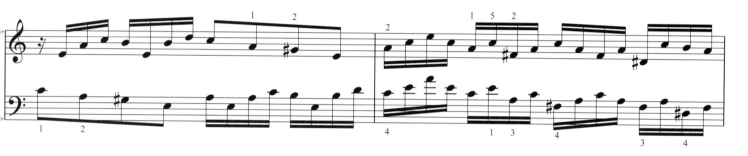

Invention No. 14 in B-flat Major
BWV 785

Johann Sebastian Bach
(1685–1750)

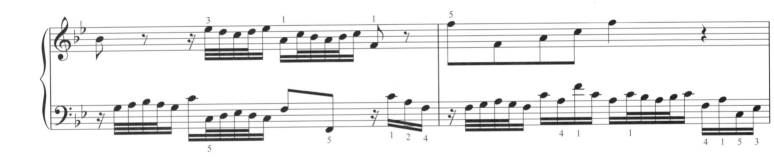

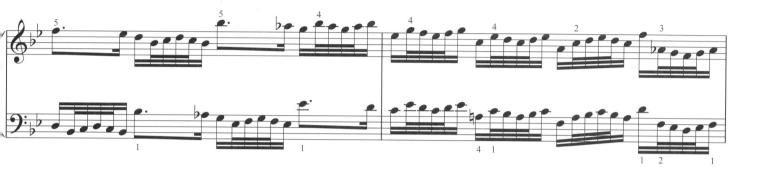

Invention No. 15 in B minor
BWV 786

Johann Sebastian Bach
(1685–1750)

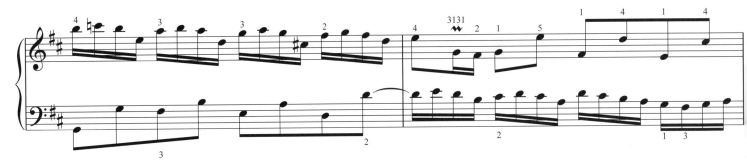

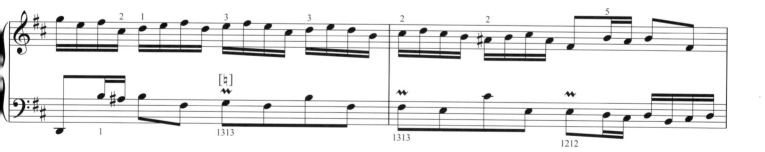

Sarabande
from English Suite No. 2 in A minor, BWV 807

Johann Sebastian Bach
(1685–1750)

[Andante sostenuto]

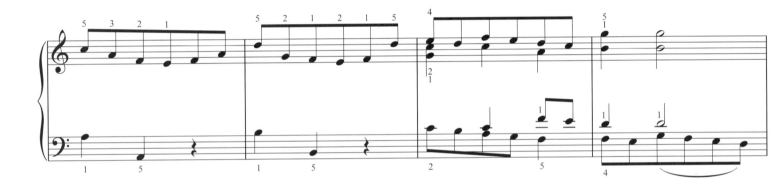

This piece has been revoiced for ease of reading for an intermediate pianist.

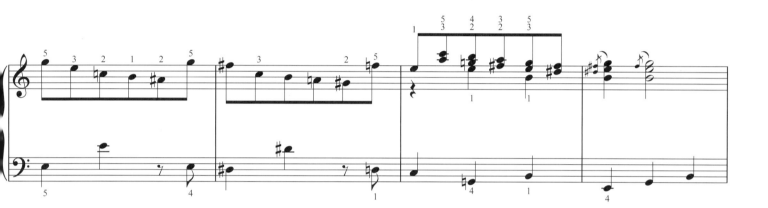

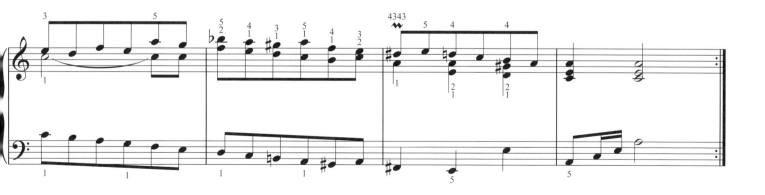

Gavotte I
from English Suite No. 3 in G minor, BWV 808

Johann Sebastian Bach
(1685–1750)

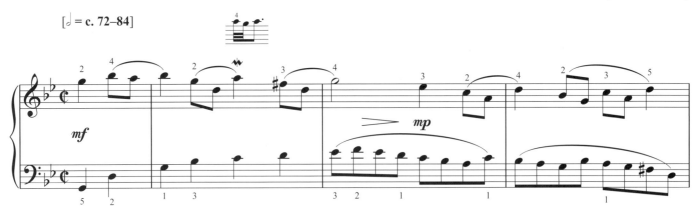

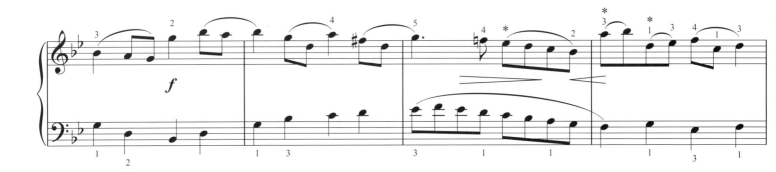

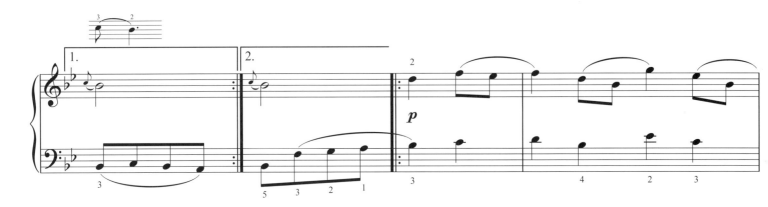

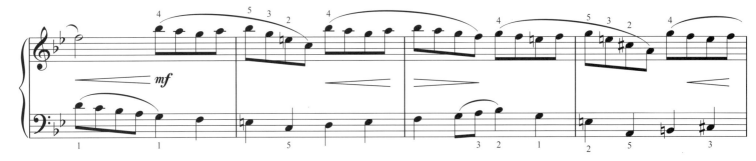

* These slur markings are in the manuscript; all other indications are editorial.

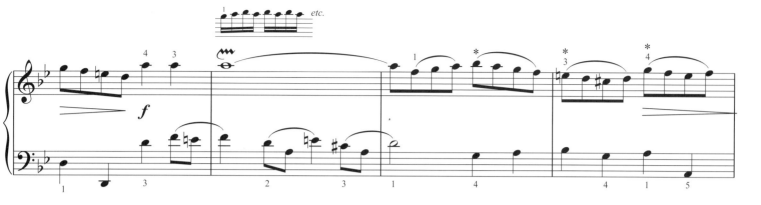

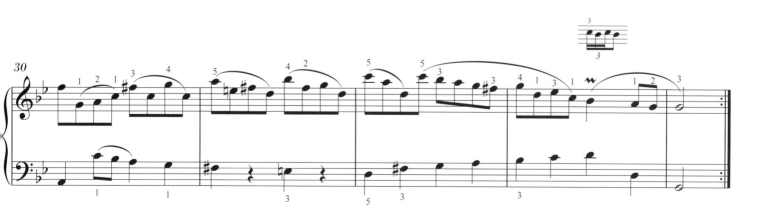

Sarabande
from English Suite No. 5 in E minor, BWV 810

Johann Sebastian Bach
(1685–1750)

* These two slurs are indicated in the manuscript.

Gavotte II
from English Suite No. 6 in D minor, BWV 811

Johann Sebastian Bach
(1685–1750)

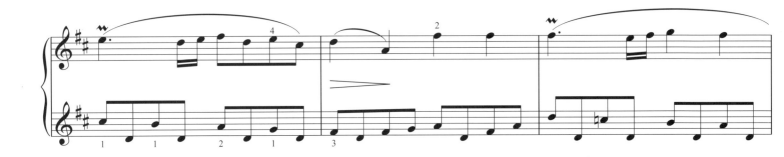

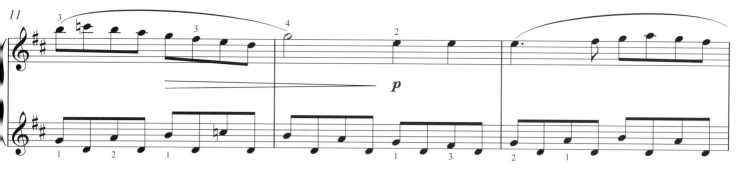

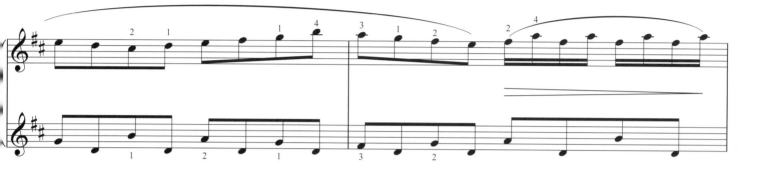

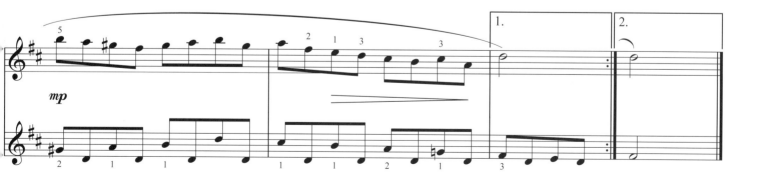

Minuet I
from French Suite No. 2 in C minor, BWV 813

Johann Sebastian Bach
(1685–1750)

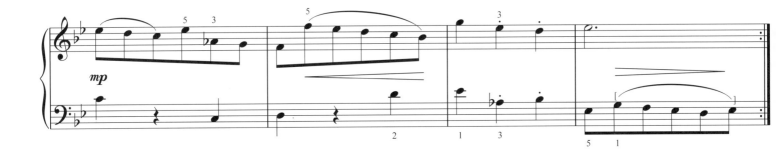

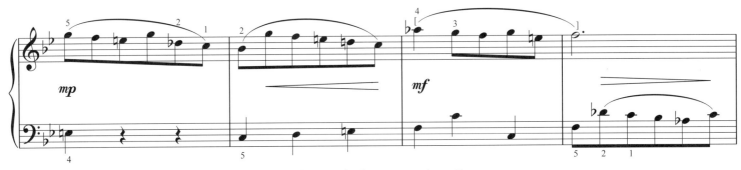

All slurs appear in the manuscript, except those in brackets, as do the staccatos in m. 7.

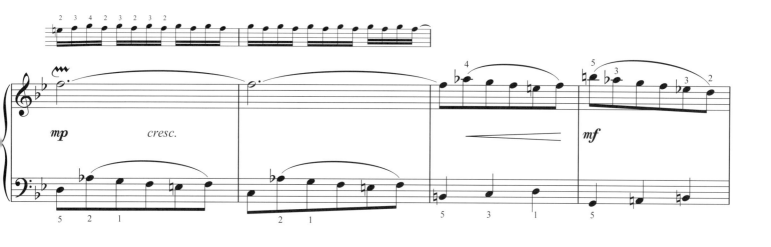

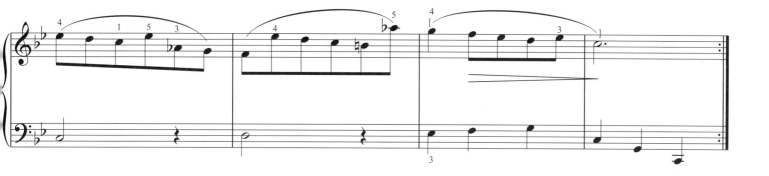

Gavotte
from French Suite No. 5 in G Major, BWV 816

Johann Sebastian Bach
(1685–1750)

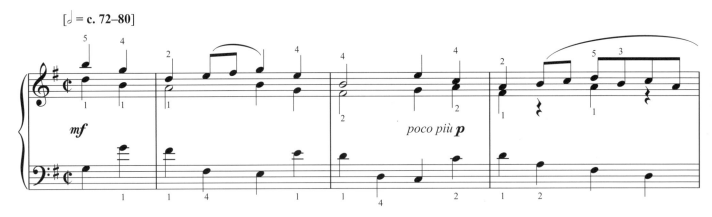

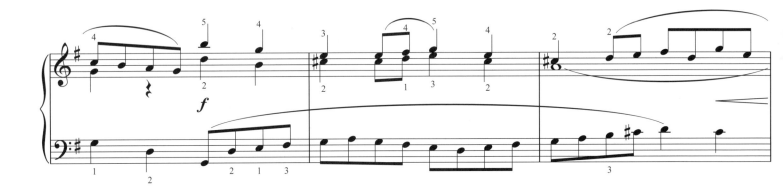

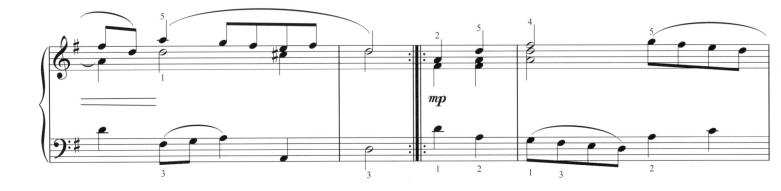

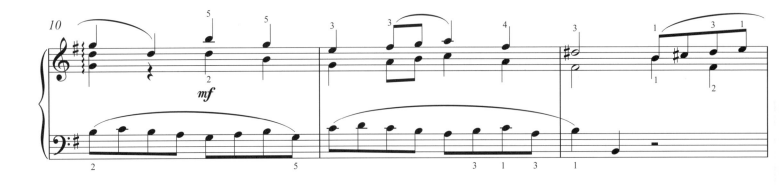

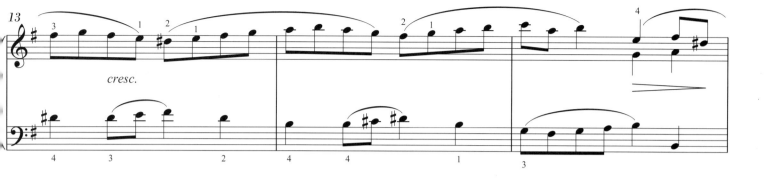

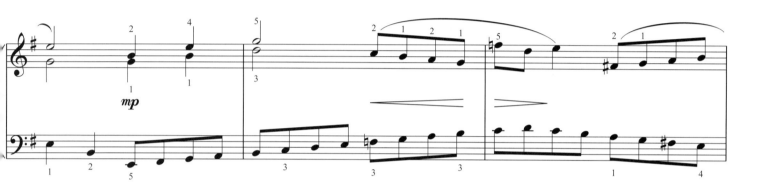

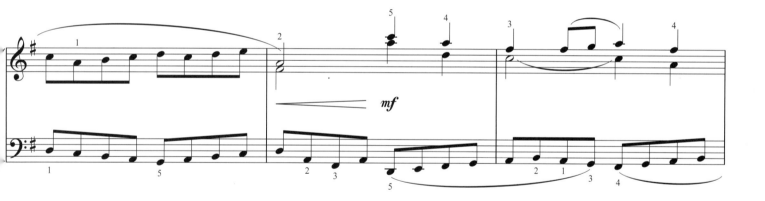

Minuet
from French Suite No. 6 in E Major, BWV 817

Johann Sebastian Bach
(1685–1750)

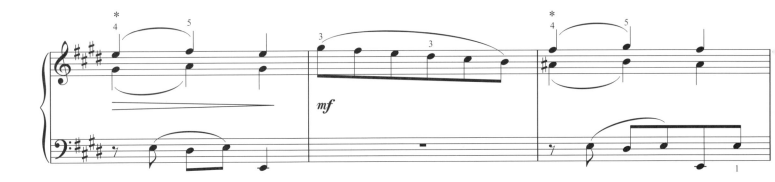

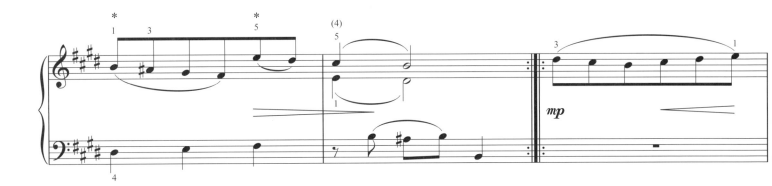

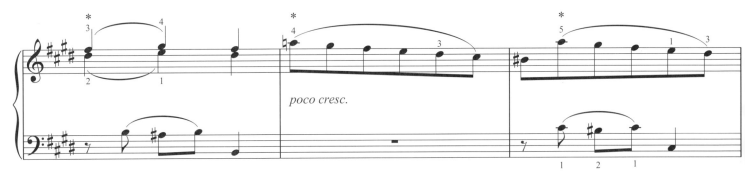

* These slur markings appear in the manuscript.

Minuet
from Overture in F Major, BWV 820

Johann Sebastian Bach
(1685–1750)

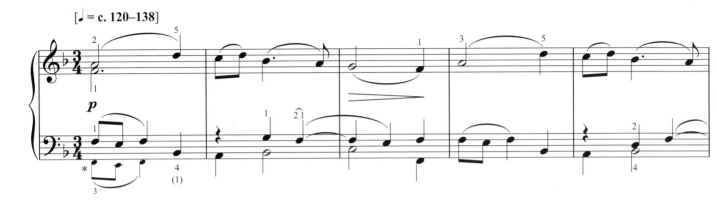

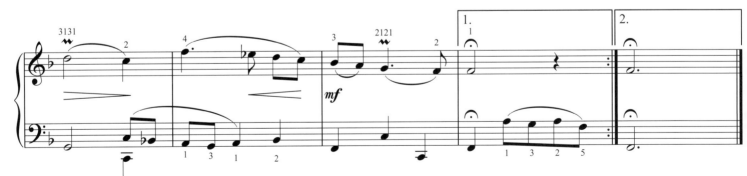

*Play small notes second time.

This page has intentionally been left blank to facilitate page turns

Gavotte en Rondeau
from Overture in G minor, BWV 822

Johann Sebastian Bach
(1685–1750)

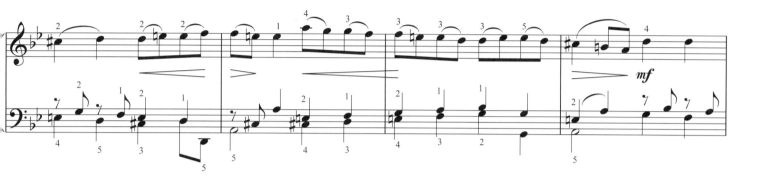

Minuet I
from Overture in G minor, BWV 822

Johann Sebastian Bach
(1685–1750)

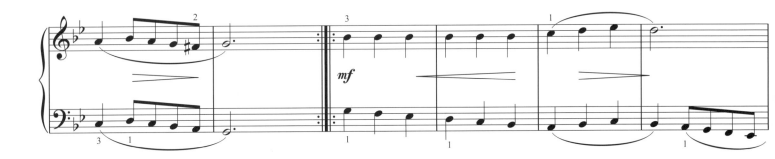

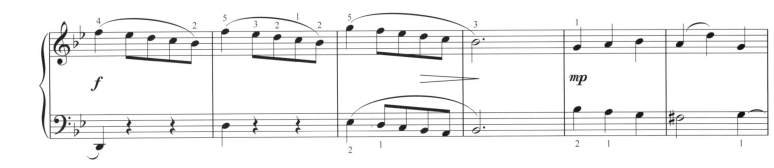

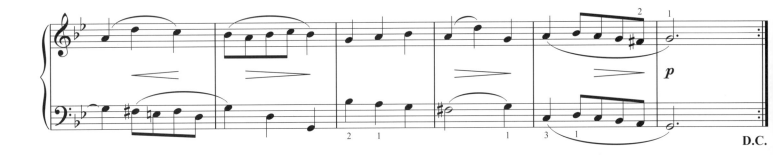

D.C.

Minuet II
from Overture in G minor, BWV 822

Johann Sebastian Bach
(1685–1750)

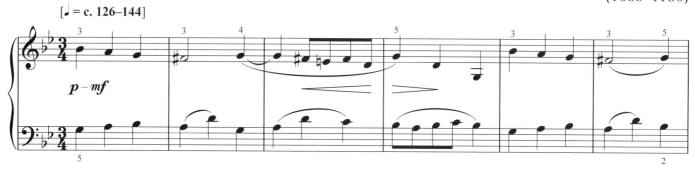

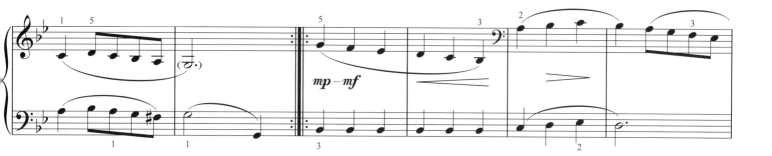

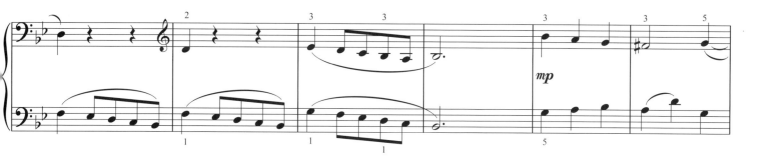

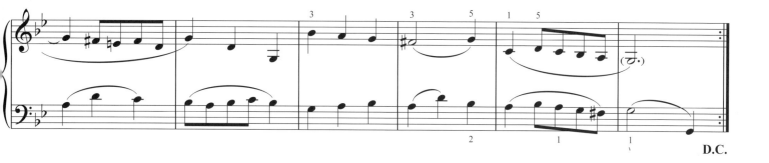

D.C.

Minuet III
from Overture in G minor, BWV 822

Johann Sebastian Bach
(1685–1750)

Musette
from English Suite No. 3 in G minor, BWV 808

Johann Sebastian Bach
(1685–1750)

* These two-note slurs appear in the manuscript.

Scherzo
from Partita No. 3 in A minor, BWV 827

Johann Sebastian Bach
(1685–1750)

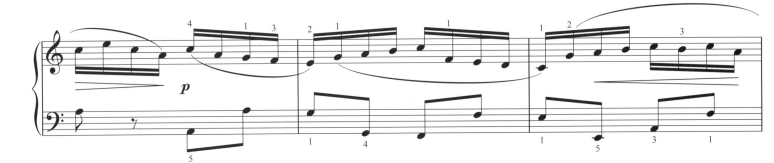

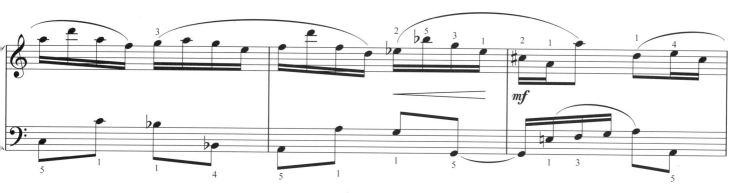

Aria

from *Goldberg Variations*, BWV 988

Johann Sebastian Bach
(1685–1750)

Andante espressivo

Bourrée
from Lute Suite No. 1 in E minor, BWV 996

Johann Sebastian Bach
(1685–1750)

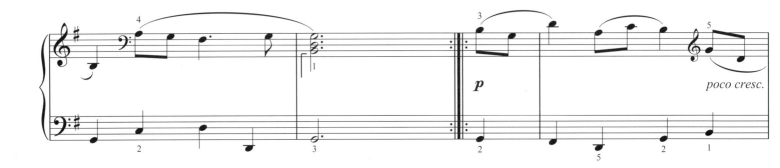

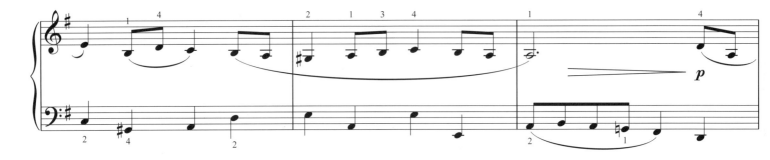

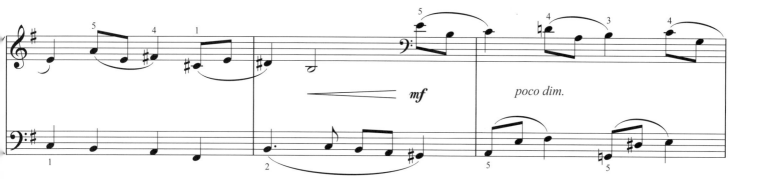

Prelude in C Major
from *The Well-Tempered Clavier*, Book I, BWV 846

Johann Sebastian Bach
(1685–1750)

[rit.]

Prelude No. 2 in C minor

from *The Well-Tempered Clavier*, Book I, BWV 847

Johann Sebastian Bach
(1685–1750)

[Allegro vivace]

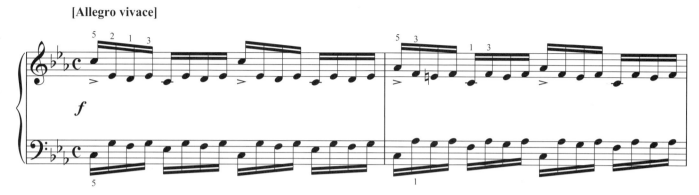

Dynamic and articulation markings are editorial suggestions.

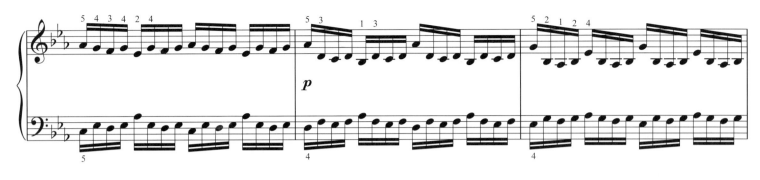

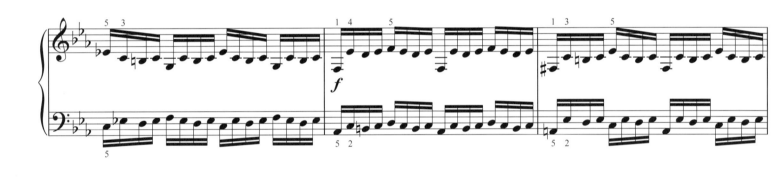

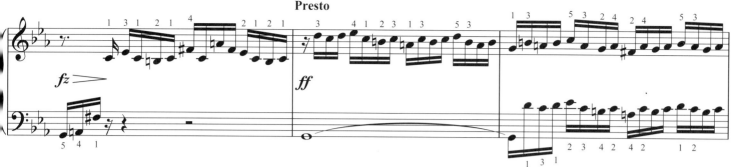

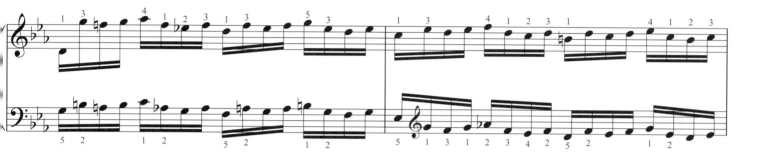

Prelude in C Major
BWV 924

Johann Sebastian Bach
(1685–1750)

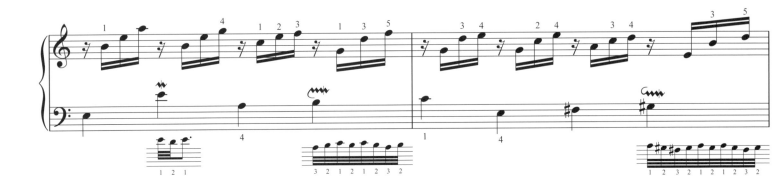

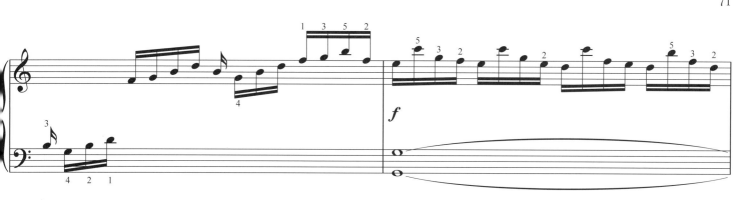

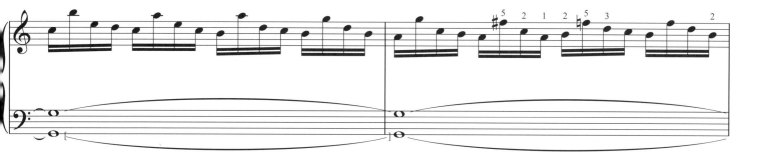

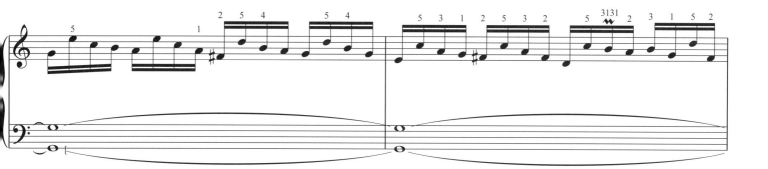

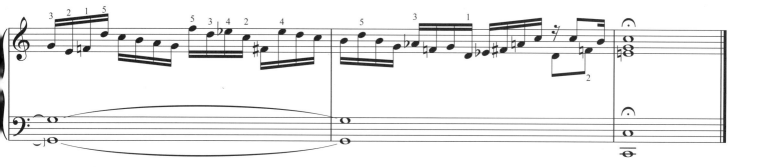

Prelude in D Major
BWV 925

Presumedly by Wilhelm Friedemann Bach
(1710–1784)

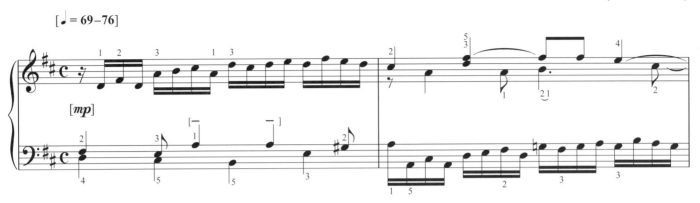

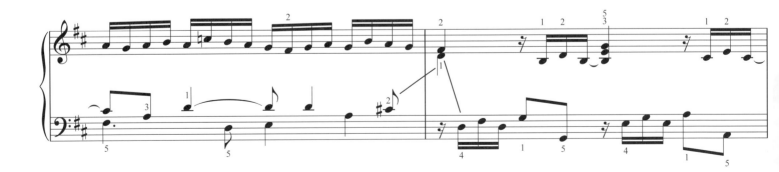

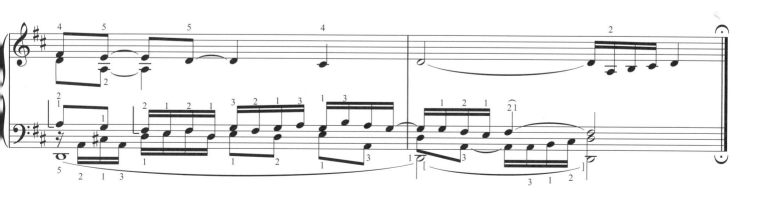

Prelude in D minor
BWV 926

Johann Sebastian Bach
(1685–1750)

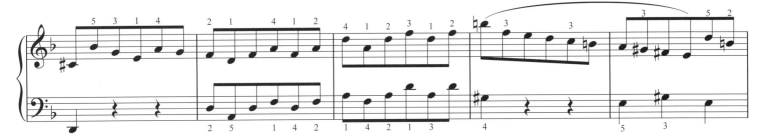

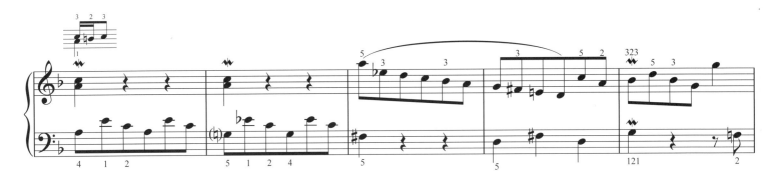

Prelude in F Major
BWV 927

Johann Sebastian Bach
(1685–1750)

[Allegro moderato]

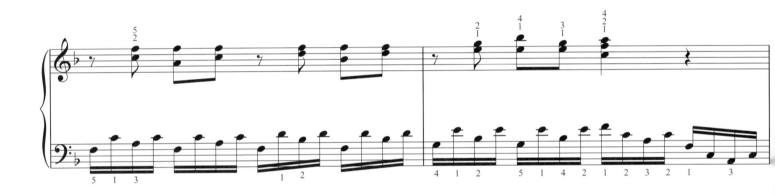

Prelude in F Major

BWV 928

Johann Sebastian Bach
(1685–1750)

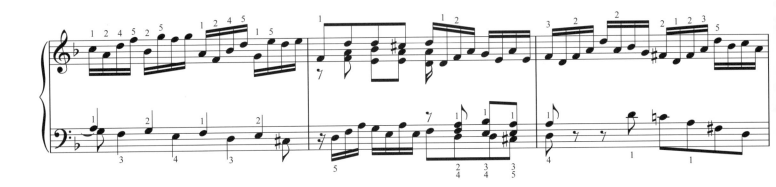

Prelude in G minor
BWV 930

Johann Sebastian Bach
(1685–1750)

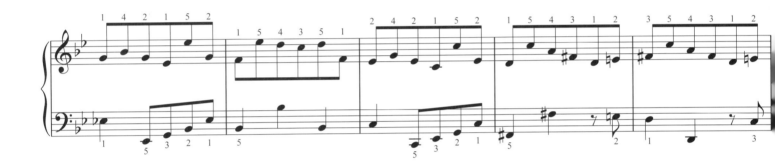

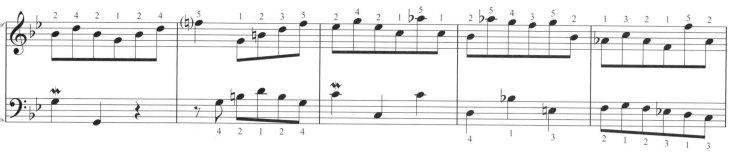

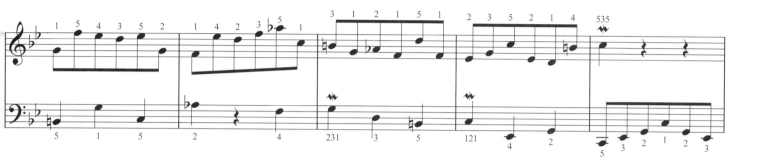

[poco rit.]

Prelude in A minor
BWV 931

Composer Unknown

Prelude in C Major
BWV 933

Johann Sebastian Bach
(1685–1750)

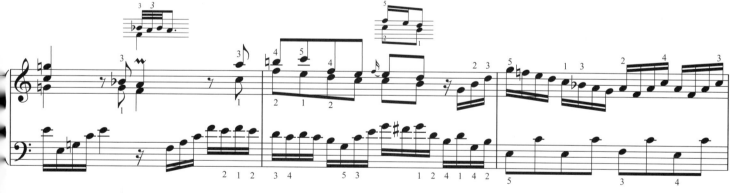

Prelude in C minor
BWV 934

Johann Sebastian Bach
(1685–1750)

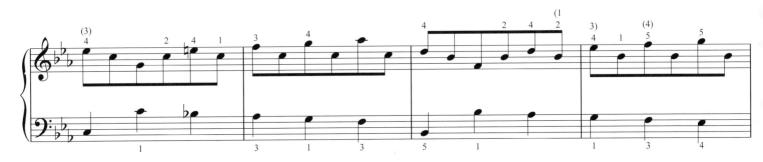

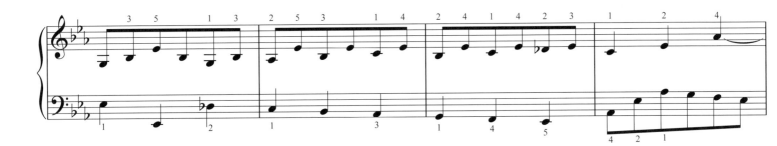

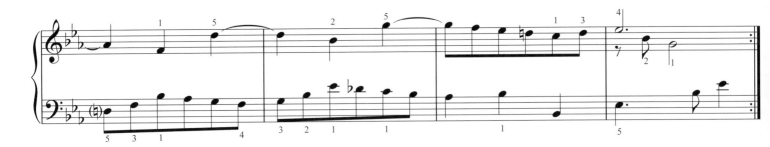

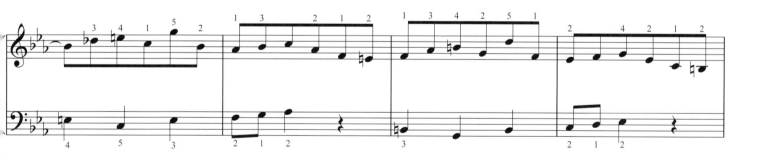

Prelude in D minor
BWV 935

Johann Sebastian Bach
(1685–1750)

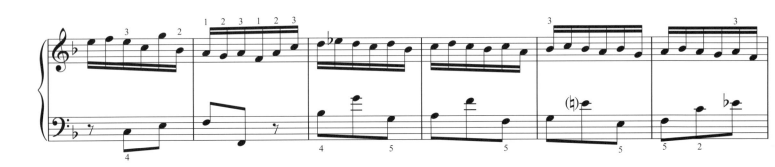

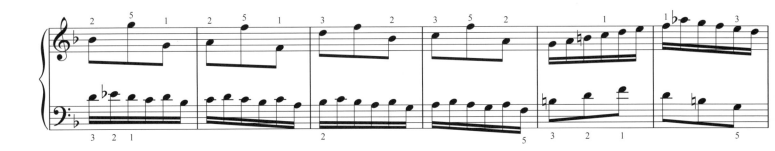

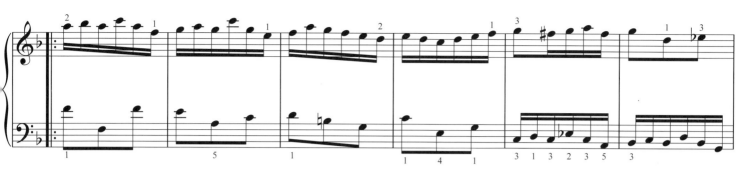

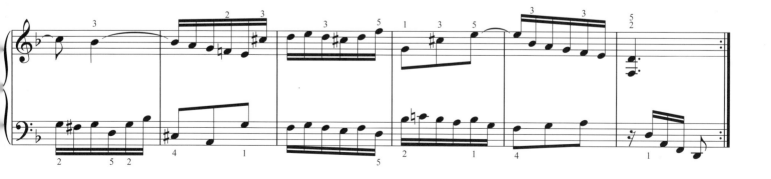

Prelude in D Major
BWV 936

Johann Sebastian Bach
(1685–1750)

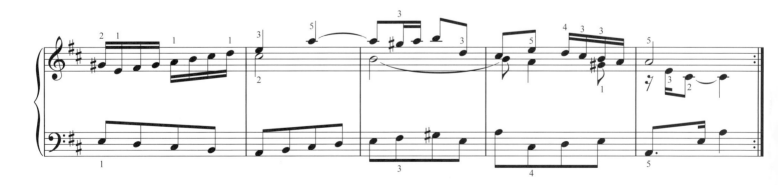

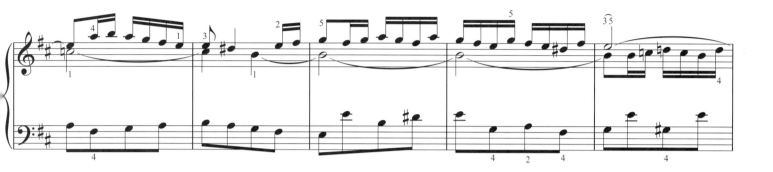

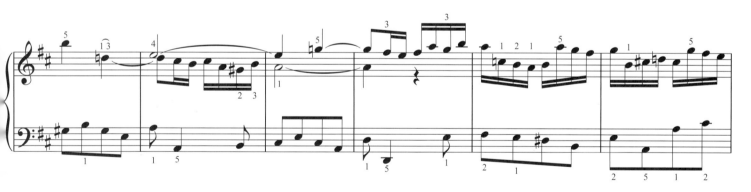

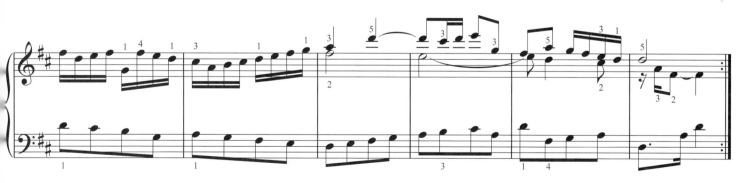

Prelude in E Major
BWV 937

Johann Sebastian Bach
(1685–1750)

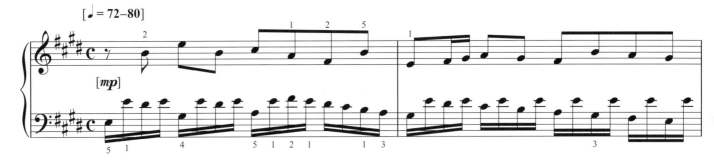

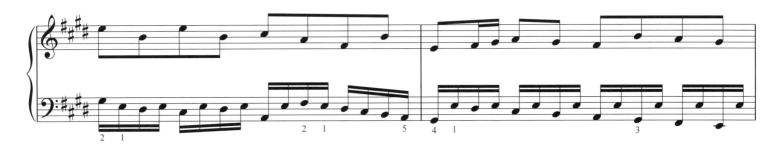

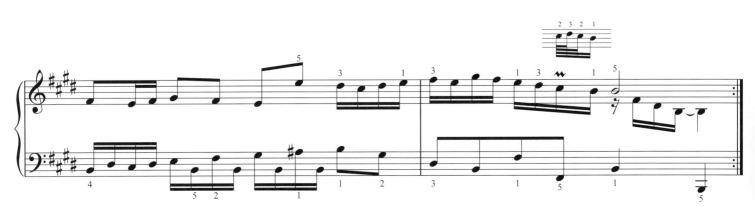

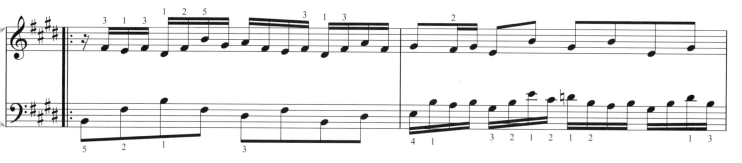

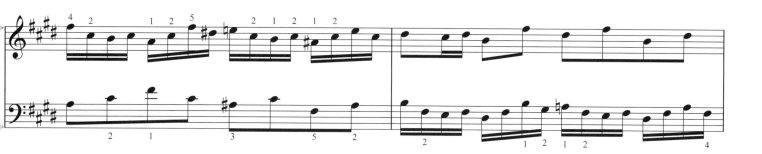

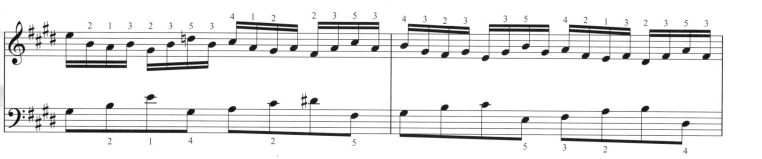

Prelude in E minor
BWV 938

Johann Sebastian Bach
(1685–1750)

[♪ = 168–192]

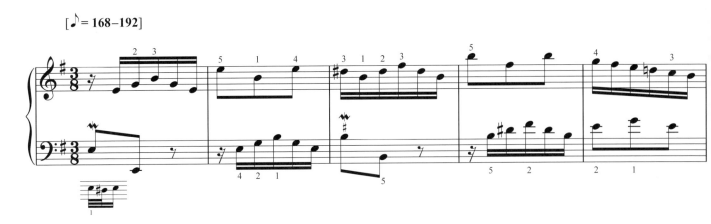

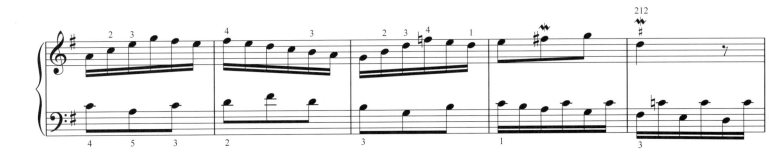

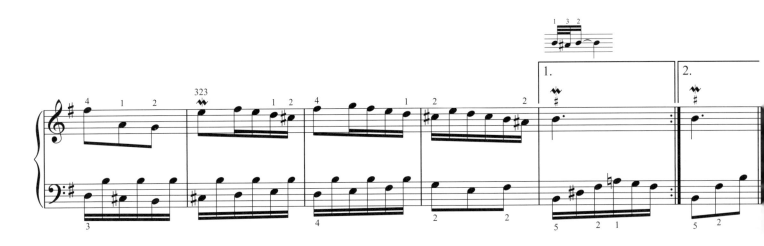

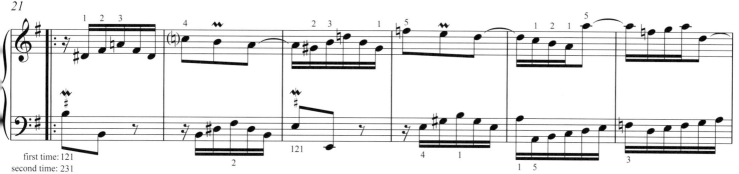

21

first time: 121
second time: 231

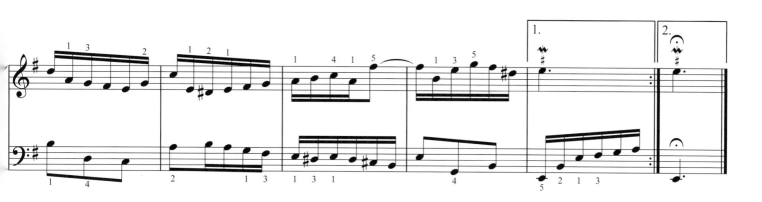

Prelude in C Major

BWV 939

Johann Sebastian Bach
(1685–1750)

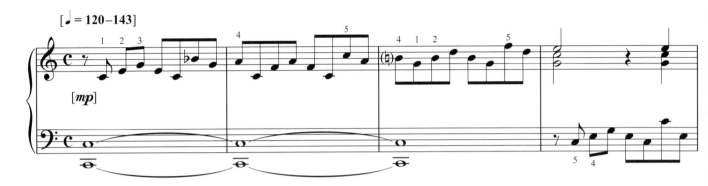

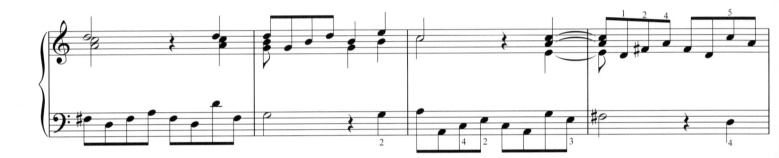

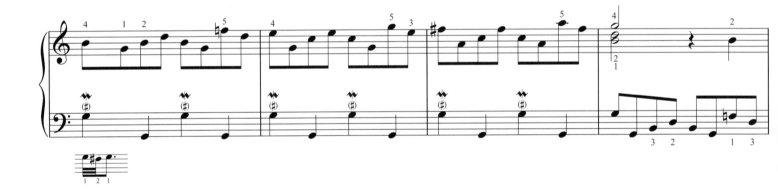

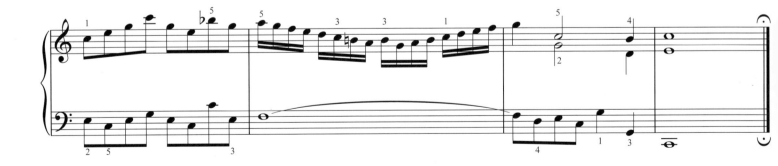

Prelude in D minor
BWV 940

Johann Sebastian Bach
(1685–1750)

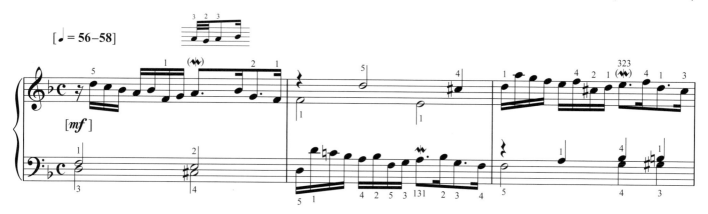

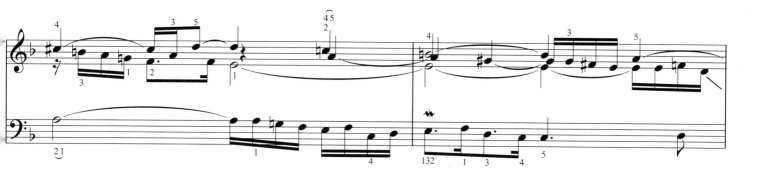

Prelude in E minor
BWV 941

Johann Sebastian Bach
(1685–1750)

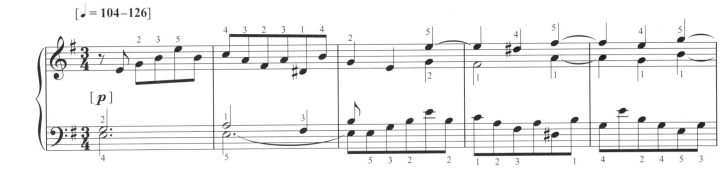

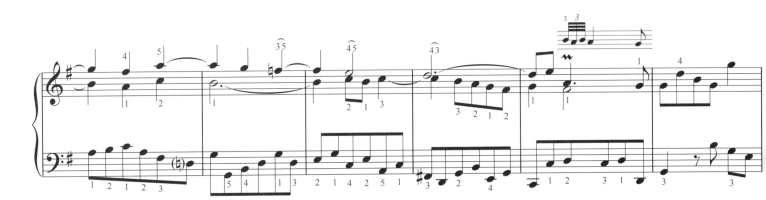

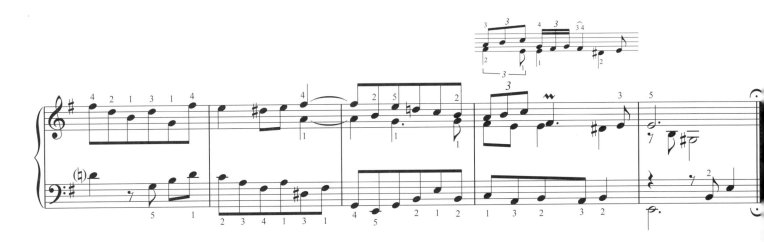

Prelude in A minor
BWV 942

Johann Sebastian Bach
(1685–1750)

Prelude in C Major
BWV 943

Johann Sebastian Bach
(1685–1750)

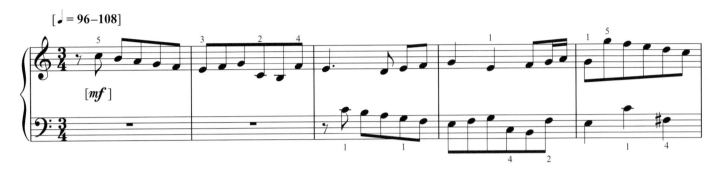

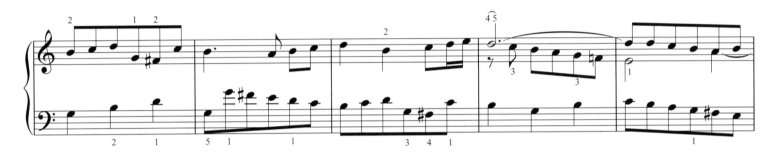

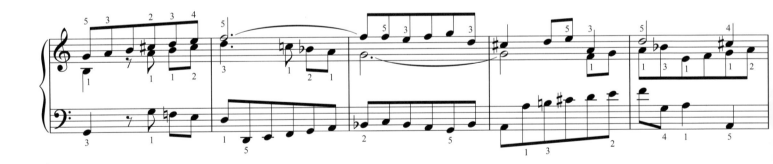

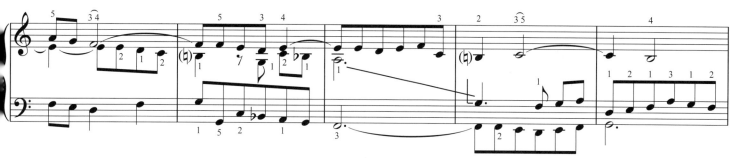

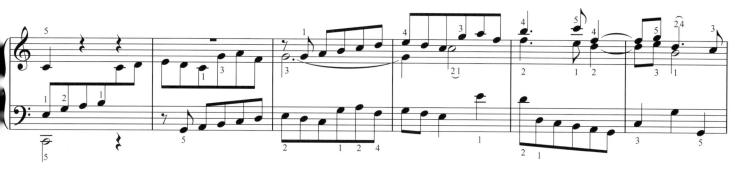

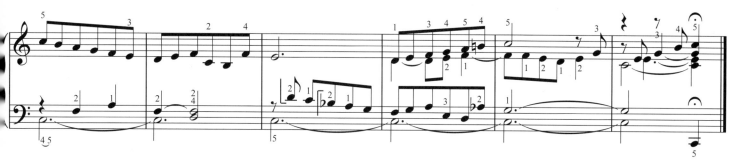

Prelude
from Suite in F minor, BWV 823

Johann Sebastian Bach
(1685–1750)

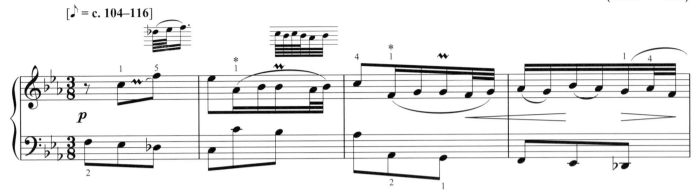

* These slur indications are found in the manuscript.

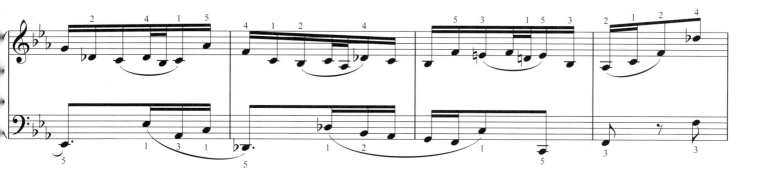

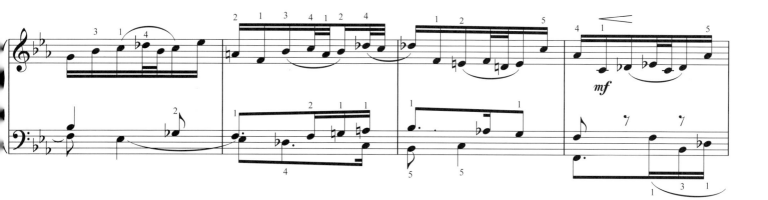

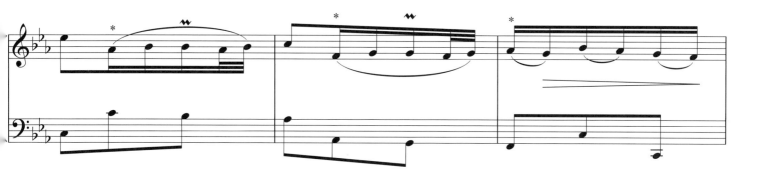

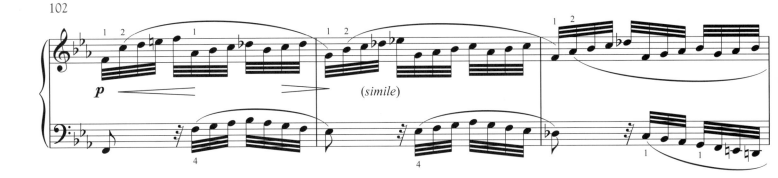

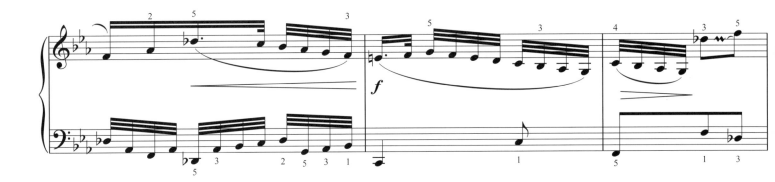

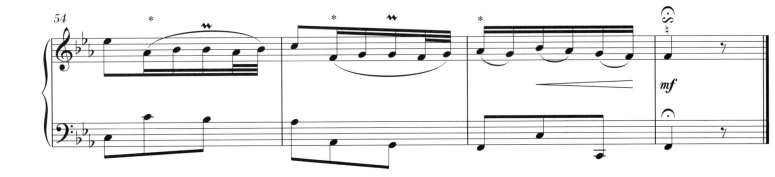

Prelude in C minor
BWV 999

Johann Sebastian Bach
(1685–1750)

[Allegro moderato]

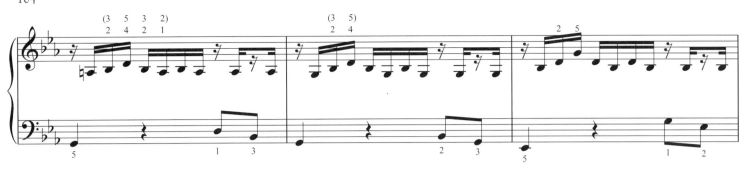

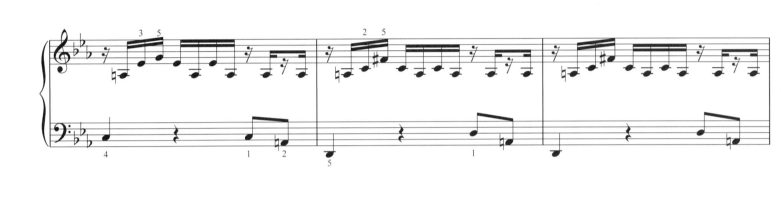

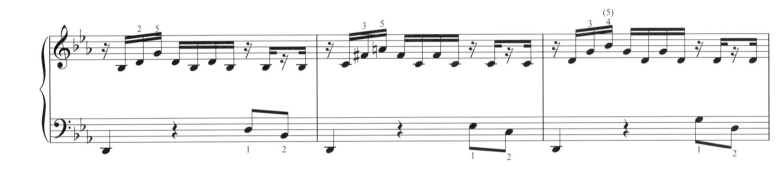

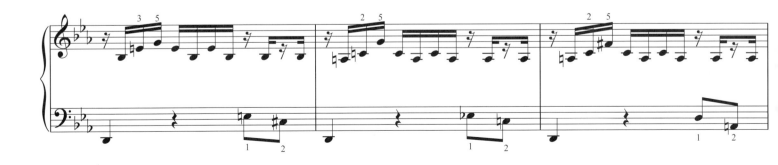

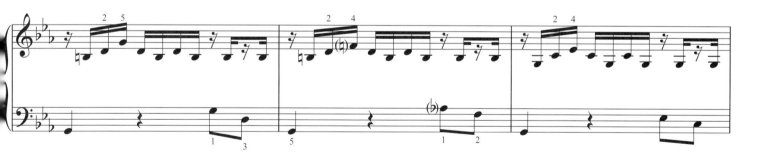